Burger King of the Dead

Also by the Author

NOVEL
Pie Man [Southeast Missouri State Press]

POETRY COLLECTIONS
Martha Playing Wiffle Ball in Her Wedding Dress
    [Encircle Publications]
Flies [Ugly Duckling Presse]
Barney and Gienka [CW Books]
The Hat City After Men Stopped Wearing Hats [WordWorks]
Watching Cartoons Before Attending A Funeral [White Pine Press]

CHAPBOOKS
Missing Persons [Encircle Publications]
Mr. Z., Mrs. Z., J.Z., S.Z. [Ugly Duckling Presse]
Bolivia Street [Burnside Review Press]
Further Adventures of My Nose [Ugly Duckling Presse]
Dennis Is Transformed into a Thrush [White Eagle Coffee Store Press]
Five-hundred Widowers in a Field of Chamomile [Portlandia Group]
Caliban Poems [West Town Press]

ANTHOLOGIES
Waking Up the Earth [Grayson Books]
Sunken Garden Poetry Festival Twentieth Anniversary Anthology
    [Wesleyan University Press]
Hecht Prize Anthology [Waywiser Press]
Warsaw Tales: A Collection of Central European Contemporary
    Writing [New Europe Writers]
Seeds of Fire: Contemporary Poetry from the Other USA
    [Smokestack Books]
Emily Dickinson Awards in Poetry Anthology [Universities West Press]
2001: A Science Fiction Poetry Anthology [Anamnesis Press]

PLAYS
My Nose and Me [A TragedyLite or TragiDelight in 33 Scenes]
My Life as a Fetus

Burger King of the Dead
Poems
John Surowiecki

GRAYSON BOOKS
West Hartford, Connecticut
graysonbooks.com

Burger King of the Dead
Copyright © 2021 by John Surowiecki
Published by Grayson Books
West Hartford, Connecticut
ISBN: 978-1-7364168-0-8
Library of Congress Control Number: 202190695

Interior & Cover Design by Cindy Stewart
Author Photo by Denise Rodosevich

For Denise and Dorothy

Self knowledge is always bad news.
—John Barth

Contents

Vodka Martini *à la* Menelaus	11
I Am a Comic Book	12
Mr. and Mrs. Fish	13
Mrs. Janecek, Inventor of the Telephone	19
My Lovely Contortionist	20
The Circe of Grants	21
Generic Animal Crackers in Indiscernible Shapes	22
Zone 6	23
Rhode Island	24
Adventures in Long Island [No. 1]: The Helpless Detectives	25
Adventures in Long Island [No. 2]: Albert's House	26
Adventures in Long Island [No. 3]: Shit-Faced at Montauk Point	27
Lorenzo Dow under my Garden	28
Clematis Grows in My Grandmother's Lungs	30
My Grandfather's Advice to Songbirds	31
Childhood Memories of the Korean War	32
Ruby and the Romantics	33
Kafka U.	34
Obit Man [*Bridgeport Post*, 1966]	35
Unrhymed Sonnet between Two Declarative Sentences [No. 1]: S.Z. Leaves for Vietnam	36
Unrhymed Sonnet between Two Declarative Sentences [No. 2]: S.Z. Departs from Troy	37
Modern Romance [Roy Lichtenstein]	38
The Vomiting Bride	39
The Helen of St. Kitts	40
Zeus in Florida: Three E-mails	42
Burger King of the Dead	44
Last Day at Price Rite [Willimantic, Connecticut]	45
Proverbs of Birdland	46
Walt's Tips on Taxidermy and Home Decor	47
Tragic Swimming Pool, Cheesy Vegas Motel	48
The Giant, Aegaeon	49

The Summer of Our Best Tomatoes	50
Elegy for Poetry	51
Adventures in Long Island [No. 4]: Elegy for a Birthday Party Magician	52
Notes on the Poems	53
About the Author	54
Acknowledgments	55

Vodka Martini *à la* Menelaus

K.'s sister says she likes hers dirty,
which means taking the silver out of it,
dimming with a lacy green fog
the sparkle of stars,
turning the icy perfection
of January into a late August swamp.

                                            It's water, after all.
Woda, wodka. Would she drink murky water? No, no,
but she's Greek. She loves olives. They ooze
the plasma of ancient enemies:
Theseus, Paris, despised Deiphobus.
As for purity, screw that! *Yia mas!*
Na zdrowie!

I Am a Comic Book

     When I was a boy of steel the universe
was made up of four elements [cyan, magenta, yellow,
black] and I was in love with every woman on Earth,
eventually only dark-rooted Mrs. Janecek
who once said it was impossible
not to think of the impossible as a kind of pornography.

     I wore purple suits, yellow ties, big fedoras.
I was the open-mouthed face at the bottom of the page:
everyone's rescue in some way rescued me.
I provided the gasps of horror,
waiting for catastrophe
as if it were a bus.

     I undid the past by running away from it
at unimaginable speeds, stretching conceits
to absurd levels: but I was
already growing up absurd.
My city leaned and wobbled.
My gangsters ran out of gas.

     I still think of myself as a comic book,
not so much its narratives anymore or its reveries
and soliloquies, but its medium,
the cheapest kind of paper,
coarse, stained, creased with the scars
of being folded and hidden away.

     And the paper has a piss-talc smell to it.
All the words are gone, replaced by
grunts and the gasps that preface getting up
and shuffling off to another room,
tired of remembering, tired of remorse,
deaf to the chatter of adventure.

Mr. and Mrs. Fish

I
MR. FISH'S HEART

It wears a scarf of thorns and sports
a circumcision's scar. It's probably on fire, too,
a cool blue flame or a briquette glowing red—a
zero-intolerant, unexplaining thing:
a carbon valentine.

Mr. Fish's ticker disappears
for days at a time, hiding like a rat
in the high grass where the old
movie theater used to be, nibbling on ancient
popcorn, pawing at ghosts of cinematic love.

Sometimes it's in his breast pocket,
inches from where it's supposed to be.
Sometimes it drops to the ground and stays there, a pear
under a pear tree, attracting impatient bees.
Sometimes it flies up, a frightened lark.

II
MRS. FISH'S TEARS

She's the one standing over us as we sleep.
Her tears fall on our exposed feet,
our folded hands, our torpid faces,
flooding our eye
sockets until they spill over.

                                            When we wake up
we think the tears are ours which leads us
to believe our lives are more miserable
than we know. We wonder when did we
become epicenters of sorrow, when

                                            did wildflowers beg
for explanations? When did lawns turn white
and crispy and mowers sleep in their sheds dreaming of
suburban women? When did storms get shoved down
the throats of things and limbs fall on us like leaflets?

                                            When did highways
shine like phonograph records and ornamental
pear trees with waxy leaves and impotent fruit
reach up instead of out, offering us nothing
in the way of shade?

III
MRS. FISH FINDS HERSELF
IN A SHORT FILM ABOUT GRIEF

She prepares a meal we know she won't eat:
honeyed carrots, spinach salad, chicken broth with orzo.
In the next scene her cat laps up butter left on the counter.
The camera follows the cat,
accompanied by a phrase on the clarinet.
At night, rainwater beading on the windowpane
is projected on her bedroom wall by the corner street lamp:
a colony of jittery cells: life beginning again.

*

She names the objects in her room he
never knew she owned. So many songs
he'd never heard her sing, books he'd never heard of,
clothes she'd worn just to annoy him, hats in a totem,
gloves reaching out. Later, the camera tracks her
on a path parallel to the one she's on.
Soon she's walking out of frame
and all we are left with are trees.

*

The camera maneuvers around boxes and towers
of books, finds a wall of photos,
mostly of her and her mother, none of him.
He was the photographer, the unseen presence,
although in one snapshot, with a lake
like a sheet of mica behind them,
his shadow, elbows flared,
rises from the center of the earth.

IV
EVENTS LEADING UP TO
THE FISHES' DIVORCE

He knows exactly how vile and low he's
become, a skunk cabbage, a cowbird,
a dog unwelcome in every house there is,
and yet he can't stop thinking of
her flawless teeth, thin ankles,
smooth heels. Her hips
are still the engines
of her flimsiest dresses.

He doesn't know how or why
but he can slip into things, solid objects, walls
mostly, watching as she showers,
on her way to a party or concert,
maybe dinner with someone with a French name,
putting in her eyes,
giving herself nails and lashes,
rubbing life into her cheeks.

V
MRS. FISH FALLS IN THE SHOWER

Her fall began at the Cape, 1966, October at its
        most ochre, a solo stumble down dunes,
sand in her cracks and creases: a gradual descent
all these years except for the time when she,
        pruning her crabapple, fell
headlong into a galaxy of red planets,

frightening a bunting on the way down
        exactly like the one she'd seen
in *Birds of North America*. Similar, she
supposed, to living on a spinning earth
        and not feeling the spin. O the
plummet is real all right, just not perceptible.

All she ever knows of it is a mild vertigo,
        a cracked tile, a gap in the grouting,
a shower pan gray-blotched from years
of dyeing, but no longer gritty as it was
        on those giddy days at the beach
when all the world was a friend.

VI
MR. FISH JUMPS OFF A CLIFF

The edge is an acrylic ripple, a *trompe-l'œil*.
Now he can see himself falling before he falls.
        Now it all becomes clear:

how his wife's feet take all summer to tan, how her body
lifts in hydraulic fashion before climax, how her heart
        leaps out of her chest

and circles her bedroom squirting blood all over
the place. He's airborne now, one arm extended,
        the other akimbo.

Her crabapple is perfectly still except for
one leaf twisting and trembling as if moved
        by a single breath.

That leaf, she thinks, that breath,
that little column of air, will be him
        for the rest of her life.

Mrs. Janecek, Inventor of the Telephone

Whenever pineapple-
shaped candies with uncertain hearts
appear in a bowl she thinks she ought
to contact Hawaii even though
she doesn't know anyone there

and whenever my sister and I thank her for
whatever kind of licorice it is
that tastes like beets
and looks like electrical wire
connections are probably made.

She likes to show us
old photos of herself,
a student at the *Politechnika*,
and when she does I want to be
a bird flying over her

reporting on her bluish wrists and the soft concentric
circles of her elbows, the milky way
of specks above her neckline
and the pale soil under the primroses
of her summer dresses.

Because of her invention
I can talk to girls anywhere in the world.
She's turned voices into tulips,
nervous breathing into orchids.
There's no reason why Juliet should ever die.

Mrs. Janecek says love is the new technology.
She lets me throw my tennis ball
against her garage wall for hours on end.
When I wave to her she always waves back.
Her laugh always begins with a smile.

When she visits my dreams she stays
a long time so I can look at every
inch of her without rushing
or glancing over my shoulder or
waiting for someone somewhere to speak.

My Lovely Contortionist

Lithuania still rages in her raisin eyes,
all those funerals without bodies,

weddings without grooms or beer-
stained uncles or beet-stained aunts,

all those places where light accuses
and one's name is the biggest lie of all.

She's my secret pretzel and sad enigma,
my heart's totem, piling herself upon herself,

strata of flesh and sequins,
a ladder of love:

toes, ankles, chin, lips. nose, eyes,
brows, forehead, bangs, crotch.

The Circe of Grant's

She said she never minded the sweet
sticky smell of the pet department. It was
where her hamsters ran in aluminum circles
and painted turtles marched up and down
their plastic *Purgatorios*. It was where she told us
about escaped parakeets falling from the sky like
unripe fruit: how only a few ever reached New Haven
to live in great budgie cities by the sea.

She was always kind to us,
extra kind to the crafty older boys
who had ideas about spitting
into the fish tanks or feeding
the mynah Blackjack gum.
She said they were good boys at heart
and invited them to visit her
any time.

Once we saw her on the street without her blue-
green smock and badge and ring of tiny keys
and we couldn't believe how beautiful she was,
how black her eyes were, like olives or onyxes,
or how gracefully her hair, freed from its netting,
settled on her shoulders. She wore lipstick and rouge
and in truth we wouldn't have recognized her at all
had it not been for the smell.

Generic Animal Crackers
in Indiscernible Shapes

A few are upside-down and appear to be in pain.
Some are pinned against the plastic wall
or struggle under the weight

of their brothers and sisters.
Suddenly we think about
mass graves and indifferent zoos

or wonder what half a rhino
might be called and whether two stumps
can be seen as four legs. Suddenly

we reflect on what a mouth really is or eyes
really are or where they might belong
on a fragment of a face.

Zone 6

> *Adieu Adieu*
> *Soleil cou coupé*
> —Apollinaire

Our silver irises ring in the void.
The rest of the garden's fine,
the pines, fine, although we're
still afraid an ICBM might drop
out of the sky and land in
the middle of our Siberians.
Meanwhile, a chainsaw
chokes somewhere and sleek
dogs eat meat in a gulp.
Wary of those crazed beasts
we take shovels with us
when we go to get the mail
and when we're tired from
digging we lean on them,
wondering if our sanguineas
will hemorrhage one day
in a new hot zone or if our blue
flags will ever find hospices of
shade before everything changes
and gardens retreat from our
ability to see them. No one will
ever know it was we who planted
those irises. The peonies are ours
too and the cherry tree and the tulip
with inexact leaves like those drawn
by children. We laid a carpet of
myrtle, imagined the reach of lilacs,
theorized what nature would be like
if it lived in the vacuum it abhors.
Now we make beds for the children
of the children of strangers or for
a drought that rises to its source and
sinks to the molten core of the earth
making dust of irises and irises,
bearded and beardless, of dust.

Rhode Island

I remember when it left New England to go
swimming on its own. From New London it looked
like a new land mass, but New London's on the Sound

not the Ocean, so it's not the best vantage point. Even when RI
goes out too far you can still feel its
salt in your lungs and its sand
in the corners of your eyes.

RI's a good swimmer and has a nautical past, which visitors
appreciate: there's an anchor on its flag and the word HOPE.
I like its no-milk chowder and wild rose bushes

which shoot magenta flowers at you in Roman-
candle fashion. And did you know there are
forty different kinds of orchid in RI
including Spring Ladies' Tresses

and the Lesser Purple Fringed Bog Orchid?
But the best thing is you can smell its heat
as it corrugates the air.

It smells like something left on the low burner
for a long time, a smell that radiates
and fills a house—the whole world for that matter.
The state that radiates. That's my idea for a slogan.

Adventures in Long Island [No. 1]: The Helpless Detectives

The man who throws bodies off the Whitestone,
delighted to see them splatter like water balloons,
has memorized every word Milton ever wrote.

He feeds bluejays oily black seeds
and drinks oily black coffee,
watching children twirl on their swings
and build castles in a sandbox
cats piss in.

We spend the day filling notebooks,
dusting for prints,
but no one really expects us to solve anything.

On the evening news we admit we're of no help at all
and hope by saying so we offer some consolation.
We do wonder, though, what those parents think their
children smell like when they go off to school and who it was
that brought death into the world and all our woe.

Adventures in Long Island [No. 2]: Albert's House

    The jets leaving JFK fly over so low
the children think they can jump up,
        grab an axle and catch a ride to Europe,

        but Albert tells them they'd soon be dead
if they did such a thing,
        frozen solid by the time they reached Bridgeport,

    little kid popsicles
stuck to the landing gear.
        And the turbulence would be such

        that they'd shake and shimmy and their
newly crystallized selves would shatter.
        It would start to snow and—guess what?—

        they'd be the snow!
If it were winter they'd be snow
        all the way down

        to the ground; if it were summer
they'd be a passing shower,
        the kind that doesn't leave a mark

        on sidewalks and roads
and barely registers as a caress or kiss
        when it touches someone's skin.

Adventures in Long Island [No. 3]: Shit-Faced at Montauk Point

I stand as on some mighty eagle's beak.
—Walt Whitman

If—at the end of the parking lot
where the flagpole clanks hollowly in the wind
and where nests of boulders hide gull wings and
the bleached plates and shards of crabs and
heaps of unidentified feet and arms and legs,
—one could drink up or gulp down the Atlantic, it
would still be where it is, but it
wouldn't be what it
                    is, an oozy Jell-O of gray fruit.
Instead it would be our barfly pal, drunk again,
his skin stretched across the world,
the stripes of his oxford shirt like lines
of longitude, his breath like trade winds,
his right hand like a cup in Cattlewash
filled with killdivil rum, his toes
tickling the toasty coast of Curaçao.

Lorenzo Dow under my Garden

I
CRAZY DOW

He lived where I live. I hear him under my tiger lilies
and day lilies which some people mistake one for the other.
He was called the Son of Thunder or just Crazy Dow:
his blood is what makes my flowers orange,
his smallpox scars are their spots. He smelled liked
fertilizer when he was alive, never bathing
or washing his clothes; his beard and hair
were never acquainted with the teeth of a comb.

II
SINS OF THE FEATHER

Someone asked him to ask the Lord to
retrieve a stolen axe and bring the thief to justice.
Zo said sure, no problemo.
In the middle of his sermon he reported the theft
and said the guilty party, a member of the congregation,
had a fluffy white feather on the tip his nose and
an instant later a dozen men made public confessions,
brushing their guilt away.

III
WHERE JESUS WALKED

The tiger lily is a true lily [*Lilium*] while
the orange day lily [*Hemerocallis fulva*] is not.
Jesus, said Zo, was well aware the day lily was also called
the ditch lily and was disparaged and belittled while the tiger

had something of the theater and hothouse
about it, tragically stooped with windswept petals.
To complicate things the Lord was also fond
of the Canadian lily

[*Lilium canadense*] which is found at the edge of
marshes, yellow as old piano keys,

although some are also orange
and have spots.

IV
ZO AMONG THE TITMICE

This was when the sky was supposed to open up
and he was supposed to ascend, assumed somehow
into a cloud-island of maga trees and pink-

frilled orchids, pearl-
white swans and friendly black dogs.
This was when eagles were supposed to peck
out his eyes and vultures gag on his lymph nodes

—not these clowny little birds with pointed heads
and zombie eyes. Who invited them?
Everyone was supposed to follow him,
a river of humanity flowing upward, weeping

in public display of scars and dents. This was when
he was supposed to learn if death had a swansong
or if too much of life had been songless for too long.

V
PEGGY

She went everywhere with him, irreplaceable until
he replaced her, shocking his flock with a request

for marital volunteers. When he drove his wagon through town,
she followed at a distance to show her humility.

He gave away everything; the only thing he left her
was a funny smell in the house. She didn't mind.

She's buried on Burrows Hill, not far
from here, where the road is lined with lilies.

Clematis Grows in My Grandmother's Lungs

Someone said the seed was a plant for the Austro-
Hungarian Empire, viable, too, sucked in with a rush
of ordinary breath, quick to find a home

in interstitial furrows before roots took hold
and shoots shot up,
lingering at throat's door,
which they did.

                                      Then, lured by the
screams of a summer picnic, out they came, purple and cream,
stippled, smooth, throwing pollen at the thickly frilled clouds,

which they more or less resembled: everyone thought they were
trumpets of some kind in some kind of end-of-the-world scenario,
but the blossoms withered in the heat, bundled in babels of vines,
and the world didn't end. It didn't even change,

although somehow and for some reason
she became a human greenhouse
and the sun no longer stopped at her skin.

My Grandfather's Advice to Songbirds

Understand that glass is death. Understand
that a song seduces and the geometries
panic reveals are rarely
places of safety.

A quivering in leaves isn't always a ruse,
but it isn't always the truth, either.
And what you see isn't, except for the one time,
the last thing you'll ever see.

Hawks and owls leave traces of themselves,
signs of the hunt, but they can't be everywhere
and they can't always be hungry for
your jelly-blood and sugary bones.

Childhood Memories of the Korean War

I was told it was a country without light,
a place where sadness and darkness
were the same thing although it took some time
to realize the connection was only
coincidental since sadness demanded sleep
and sleep never came except when
it was too late, when the throat rattled and breath
smelled like nail-polish remover.

I was told light was important to heroes.
They were born in it or revealed by it. They assumed
they would chase it all their lives,
but light had its own enzymes and acids
and sometimes it hid in bright empty rooms
where families drank ginger ale
and ate saltines in semicircles
of armless chairs.

Ruby and the Romantics

As it turns out we don't have much of anything.
We used to have something, but we don't anymore.
What we have left is a mockery of what little we had.

Love never brought the joy we thought it would
or they said it would and what we shared was what
we gave each other when we were both

down on our luck. Many of us have lived with pain
none of us can begin to describe.
It's all come crashing down, hasn't it?

We were never golden or made of light.
Our day came and went and won't ever come again.

Kafka U.

For Barry Shapiro

Going to college was supposed to be like living in
one of the deserts frequented by St. Jerome,
but as it turned out, Shap, we were right at home

among the saguaros. We dated coeds
who thought disagreements, like hair,
could always be ironed out.

We metamorphosed into moles
and the moles became bedridden beetles.
Then the beetles became professorial dogs

and the dogs apes screeching for a heart
and the apes wrens with hollow bones
and the wrens Heraclitus himself

who said nothing stays still or the same,
nothing lives without becoming something else: only
self-satisfaction, being static, is ever punished.

Then Jerome moved off campus, the women
dumped us, the saguaros waved their handless arms
and we graduated.

Obit Man
[*Bridgeport Post*, 1966]
For Richard Belzer

I
He had waxy teeth and ate sardines for lunch.
We thought he smelled like death, as any obit man should,
but it was really just the fish.

II
A true obit, he said, should be thicker
than the Yellow Pages and written by a poet,
a miscellany of elegies and laments and tragedies

that adhered to time-honored conventions,
certain phrases in a certain order: nothing crude
or excessive, nothing guessed at.

III
And an obit had to have a feeling for survivors,
the brother-in-law from Yonkers
whose collision repair shop was doing okay

or the crazy aunt who glanced now and then
into the heart of eternity and saw
that dying took all sorts of turns

and spit out—in eruptions
of insets and hot type—
experiences we all could share,

gray delights and golden miseries,
war and the sudden glorious end of war,
poverty and the bewilderment of plenty.

Unrhymed Sonnet between Two Declarative Sentences [No. 1]: S.Z. Leaves for Vietnam

Men from other wars drive him to the station.

He wonders which one will visit his father,
bring him his groceries and L&Ms and vodka,
which one will keep an eye on his useless brother,
which one will drive the trash bags to the dump
and get the deposit on the quarter keg,
wheezing even now and still spitting out foam.
As a boy he liked walking the tracks so he knows
ahead of time what he'll see out the train window:
the rug outlet store, the old kosher slaughterhouse,
the brick bones of the abandoned lamp factory.
He'll see bittersweet helixing into the sky,
toilet-seat mushrooms, a patch of sunchokes—
guileless yellow faces among the fallen trees
—but after that he won't recognize a thing.

He waves, the train pulls away, he finds a seat.

Unrhymed Sonnet between Two Declarative Sentences [No. 2]: S.Z. Departs from Troy

The VA hospital is a great ship made of brick.

The sea of lawn it overlooks is the sea itself.
Behind him are charred walls and walls of flame
and a softball field no one's played on in twenty years.
In the last photo taken of him he's sitting
on a chair outside the cafeteria holding a bag
of chips and a can of Diet Coke. His hair
looks like a spray of fountain grass. His lips
glisten with grease. His eyes are the blue-white
of fat-free milk. A mole on his cheek is actually
a fly. Around the bend, the world begins again.
Golden women entice him with bowls of spices
and rows of steaming pies, but they no longer
look to him for protection. The wind picks up.
His hair flies back. The fly is blown off his face.

Land birds circle and complain and are left behind.

Modern Romance
[Roy Lichtenstein]

OH JEFF...
I LOVE YOU, TOO...
BUT...

It's 1963 and B. and I have spent the night together.
Just talking. Honest. What I learn is how ambitious love is,
how it blossoms in grad school and other antechambers
of the better-paying professions.
And yet I burn, I pine, I perish.
But B. only smiles. Apparently
love-in-idleness is no longer picked and dejuiced.
No more *le coup de foudre*
and assorted charming misadventures.
Deep sighs are not allowed. The same goes for
gushing and stifling attentiveness.
Looking at the moon is OK, but not mooniness.
Dreams are fine, but not dreaminess.
Love isn't what you can live on anymore.

I KNOW HOW YOU
MUST FEEL, BRAD...

Joy's a meteor that hisses and crackles and is gone,
not a comet that hangs in the sky like a scarf on a hook.
Some say joy doesn't even exist,
so make of it what you will:
no one seems to care one way or the other.
In *La voix humaine*, ELLE spends
most of the time on the phone
begging her lover to come back to her.
He doesn't and she strangles herself with the cord.
Well, what's a girl to do in a wireless age?
Of all the varieties of pain in the world,
love's is the mildest. It doesn't disfigure or cripple.
It breaks hearts, but doesn't stop them.
It doesn't metastasize.

The Vomiting Bride

Our most reverent whispers fill the hall,
    our hum, our hymn to her, so stoically heroic
as orange-pink fluid gushes through her fingers

and forms a map of ancient Greece on her boddice.
    Macedonia appears, Peloponnesus grows dark,
Attica overcomes golden-seamed Achaea.

Islands pop up: Naxos, Lesbos, faraway Ithaca
    where Penelope, sick to her stomach,
makes and unmakes and makes again.

The Helen of St. Kitts

I
HELEN HERSELF

Was there ever an appetite so appetizing?
Scullery maid of honor, then off
to cooking school to earn a paper hat.
That was when I, inhospitable bastard,
stole her away. We spent our best
years in bed, making a bed of everything,
usually off-center and off-fulcrum
by our tree of carved hearts.

                        And when
we swam it was among jellyfish and grunts,
my hand like a paddle against
the hot swirling current of her discharge.
We never counted days or named them.
We argued, were contrite.
Our children looked like types of fudge:
chocolate, divinity, penuche.

II
HELEN AGAIN

Once I was her dreamboat and ace in the hole, now I'm
her twitch and bad tooth, her sunburned
nipples, her silent vapor
and brittle nails.
I walk like a policeman through her dreams.
I see other men's faces between her legs.
But I'm her orangery despite it all,
her cauldron of futures.

                    Her thigh is my
resting place, her toes my Jordan almonds.
I make sugar water for her hummingbirds.
I grow horseradish
for her shrimp cocktail,
huge leaves with holes in them.

I write a poem and then I say:
This? This is for you.

III
HELEN'S NIECE (A NURSE)

She must think of me as *her* Paris whose white-
hot rivet keeps hissing near her heart.
She wipes up old spunk
and spittle and dusts off the old boys as they
go on and on about the war.
                                            O
this caved-in chest won't turn her stomach,
nor these rooster legs, nor these purses of fat

here and there,
nor this testicle the size of a cupcake.
I must be the perfume of her idle thoughts.
She needs to help me pee or
watch my tongue silver in the moonlight.
She needs to feel the hard leather of my skin
against the soft silk of hers. There's the rub.
I do bewitch her.

Zeus in Florida:
Three E-mails

I
Well, has she aged much?
a lot? at all?
Is she gray and infirm
like everyone else
in this goddam
anaconda-ridden place?
Maybe beauty transcends age,
maybe *her* beauty transcends beauty.
I still see her collecting shells
on the beaches of Troy, always
a charmer, always kind
to maids and waitresses,
guards and soldiers,
cooks and seamstresses:
the human furniture
she never wanted.

II
It was a younger universe
back then, the younger
the wronger. The sun
was a child running
in circles, the earth a
dancer spinning in place.
These days all I do is
get my colon checked
and my teeth cleaned.
And when I see a young
woman smiling I think:
Is she smiling at me?
Or is she smiling to herself
and I just get in the way?
No matter: I'm all out
of metamorphoses.

III
When does eternal hair
turn gray and undying
skin crack and wither?
When do infinite ears get
weighed down by the
heft of tragedies?
I have no news for anyone.
Life belongs to strangers
who leave me to my kidney
stones and soggy lungs.
Sometimes the world spins
and I have to hold on for
balance. Sometimes I don't
know what month it is
or whether Persephone
is coming or going.

Burger King of the Dead

And Anticlea came, whom I beat off
—Ezra Pound, *Canto I*

The dead are driven wild by the broiling meat
and soon the line is out the door. I don't recognize her at first
but when I do I tell her the lie mothers wait all their lives
to hear: that everything's going to be all right when nothing
$\qquad\qquad\qquad\qquad$ will ever be all right again.

Her days had drifted away, kites over a blustery sea.
Her tomatoes had dropped into the world never to be eaten.
What do I know about faithfulness and grief and sorrow?
What are my voyages and monsters compared
$\qquad\qquad\qquad\qquad$ to her islands of loneliness?

Last Day at Price Rite
[Willimantic, Connecticut]

What we're seeing is a glimpse of the end of things.
Melon bins are missing and the piles of buck-each
avocados have vanished. No earth-
smelling potatoes either
or Spanish onions as round
                        and white as softballs:

the whole place is a big infinite nothing,
an indoor prairie of empty shelves and perches,
warm freezers and naked pyramids.
All that's left are cans of pigeon peas,
oval tins of sardines, jugs of Jamaican kola
    shockingly yellow.

Most of all we miss the light,
the stalking brilliance overhead. Now everything
has a shadow: now light eddies and spirals.
The cashier—laid off but working, there but not there—
waits for us in the express lane and coldly accepts
    our handful of coins.

Proverbs of Birdland
For Denise

A junco is a bluebird in a black-and-white movie.

A robin's song chaperones the morning and evening star.

Your song is like the goldfinch's, hesitant and shy.

A catbird is a mimicking not a mocking bird.

The vulture's neck looks like an alto sax.

The hearts of men and women can't be seen
and their breathing takes the form of a cloud;
the finch shows no breath
and its heart is painted on its breast.

A titmouse's eyes look like pips: snake eyes.

A female cardinal and a male waxwing are made of velvet.

Darting chickadees evade invading raindrops.

Hummingbirds search all of Panama
for the rigid red flowers you hang in the holly
and the nectar you brew on the stove.

Sparrows are brown because the world is.

Wrens are streaked like cinnamon rolls.

The owl that swims in a pond starves in the rain.

Frigate birds are knives through books as well as air.

Doves creak like doors when they exit.

Jays squawk, crows cackle, warblers warble
and you laugh your lovely laugh
talking to your sister on the phone.

Walt's Ideas on Taxidermy and Home Decor

It's a shame if the great horned didn't hover
over the sofa with wings at max for a kind
of "gathering-in effect"— its glass eyes
zeroed in to every jelly-eye in the room. And
it ain't just a room anymore: it's a cemetery.
You'll want your visitors to swear they hear
noises: every screech and howl, every hiss
and growl, every soft lurch toward dinner.
Maybe even Eden awaits: dove and hawk
backlit and agreeable. As for the wee-er
beasties, you're on your own: fox trotting,
rainbow arching, songbirds just mouthing
the words, copperhead out on a limb, raven
a Y-cut of dark matter, bobcat smiling two-
penny nails, big beheaded buck wondering
what a goddam color scheme can possibly
        mean to the goddam dead.

Tragic Swimming Pool, Cheesy Vegas Motel
For Vanessa and John

The maid says another maid recently drowned
        in the deep end, clawing at
        leprous walls, swallowing
        the radioactive limeade,
                dreaming of a million-
        dollar payoff from the slots. *Mala suerte!*
        You swim, you drink her, she says,

nodding at the fishfood-murky water,
        but there's no time for a dip.
        We have a red eye to catch
                and a 7-Eleven to stop at.
        You two get bean burritos to go.
        I get packaged salami
        fanned out like a hand of cards.

The Giant, Aegaeon

> *And the empire like all empires*
> *seemed eternal*
> —Zbigniew Herbert

His arms have the strength of a hundred arms,
his brain holds the memories of fifty brains.
He works all day in the cold-cellar,

guardian of kegs and six-packs, advisor to
promotional pirates and surfers,
leprechauns and Christmas elves. At noon

the world lingers in his window, half in and half out
of a linden's half shade. As a boy he saw workhorses
lowered into the Wieliczka mine and he wept

knowing the beasts would never see the sun again.
In the salt cathedral he was usher and security guard.
On the surface

even sulfurous air is sweet to an underground man.
No matter where you are there are trees
with spinning leaves and weeds with pretty

blossoms and roots that crack stone
and there are birds that refuse to be silent
and a horizon that marks an end to it all.

The Summer of Our Best Tomatoes
In memoriam: G.T.

When he was officially declared sane he moved in
with us, helping with the kids and the garden,

tilting his straw hat against the sun the way
patients did at the institution. It was our last

summer together, the summer of the big yellow
spider, the squash that looked like Freud,

the flat beans that grew longer
than the Empress Dowager's nails.

It was the summer of kohlrabi and Japanese
watermelon when the cat survived the fan belt

and chamomile bloomed in the field next to the
basketball court so that in the afternoon it smelled

as if it were time to go to bed. It was the summer
of the blue piano and our biggest Big Boys.

At dinnertime they leapt into our open hands
—and how everyone marveled at them,

so plump and red and not a blemish on them.
It was shame to cut them open.

Elegy for Poetry

In memory of Joan Joffe Hall
poet, teacher, friend

I
In poems nothing always becomes something,
word-birds become real birds, word-cats
real cats, word-men and -women
real men and real women whether alive

or dead, named or nameless,
sick or healthy,
en route or in place, in love
or in unspeakable pain.

II
A poem is a house where doors are missing locks,
windows are missing glass,
walls are made of glass
so you can wave to someone in the next room

and that person can wave back.
Visitors come and go as they please
stealing silverware
and leaving mud on the carpet.

III
Poems continue to be submitted, rejected, accepted,
online or in print [page 1,489 of the summer issue],
read at readings, read in bed, lunch poems, sullen sonnets,
crafty odes, poems of despair, of love, of labor and loss,

poetry that makes nothing happen or nothing
much, poetry of imagined lands, of innocence
and experience, heaven and hell: but you know, Joan,
it's just not the same anymore.

Adventures in Long Island [No. 4]: Elegy for a Birthday Party Magician

You should know that in a little while he'll be gone,
this time to a room that's too bright for shadows.
He won't return.

His life is a river that has
meandered itself at last to stillness:
you must sense his disappointment where you are.

If you think he still has power over you
it's because you still grant it to him.

Can't you see how ridiculous he is, a cloud
of red smoke, a bag of corny tricks?
Nothing comes from nothing.

Nothing in the wind pushes
against your coat as you walk to school.
Belief is ignorance,

amazement laziness, applause
a gesture of surrender.

Better to learn how something
is done: enchanted things become
more enchanted once they are explained.

He's already shrunk to your size. He wets his bed.
He lives in a room of board games and photo albums
and chamfered corners. Where are his powers now?

Where is his magic? My darlings, please,
no more mysteries and no more lies.

Notes on the Poems

"Ruby and the Romantics"
A rhythm-and-blues group out of Akron, Ohio. Their big hit was "Our Day Will Come" in 1963.

"Lorenzo Dow under My Garden"
Lorenzo Dow, a well-known 19th-century preacher and firebrand, lived for a time in the Hope Valley section of Amston, Connecticut.
Crazy Dow, as he was called, conducted gospel meetings throughout the country, often attracting thousands of followers.

"Zone 6"
On a plant hardiness map, Zone 6 stretches across the middle of the United States, from Rhode Island to Washington.
Our Siberians refers to Siberian irises. *Sanguineas* and *blue flags* are also irises.

"The Giant, Aegaeon"
In Greek mythology, Aegaeon (a.k.a. Briareus) was a giant with a hundred arms and fifty heads. He and his brothers assisted the Olympians in their victory over the Titans and served as security guards when Zeus banished the Titans to the underground regions.
Salt cathedral: In the Wieliczka salt mine in Poland, miners carved an entire cathedral out of the salt.

"The Summer of Our Best Tomatoes"
tilting his straw hat against the sun: Patients using Thorazine were told to avoid unnecessary exposure to sunlight.

About the Author

Burger King of the Dead is John Surowiecki's sixth full collection of poetry; he is also the author of seven poetry chapbooks. He is the recipient of the Poetry Foundation Pegasus Award for verse drama, the Pablo Neruda Prize, the Washington Prize, a Connecticut Poetry Fellowship, a silver medal in the Sunken Garden National Competition, and other literary awards. His novel, *Pie Man*, won the 2017 Nilson Prize for a First Novel.

John has a daughter, Vanessa; a son, John Edward; and three grandsons: Jerzy, Eddie and Ishmael. He lives in Hebron, Connecticut, with his wife, Denise.

Acknowledgments

AMP: "Adventures in Long Island [No. 3]: Shit-Faced at Montauk Point," "Clematis Grows in My Grandmother's Lungs," "Ruby and the Romantics." *Anastamos:* "Mrs. Fish's Tears," "Mr. Fish's Heart." *Cider Press Review:* "The Vomiting Bride." *Connecticut Review:* "The Circe of Grants." *Connecticut River Review:* "Obit Man [*Bridgeport Post*, 1966]." *Front Range Review:* "I Am a Comic Book." *Here: a poetry journal:* "Last Day at Price Rite [Willimantic, Connecticut]." *Mount Hope Review:* "The Summer of Our Best Tomatoes." *Nimrod International Journal:* "Kafka U." "The Helen of St. Kitts." *RHINO:* "Vodka Martini à la Menelaus." *Slant:* "Adventures in Long Island [No. 4]: Elegy for a Birthday Party Magician." *The Halcyone:* "Lorenzo Dow under My Garden." *The Florida Review:* "Rhode Island." *The Scream Online:* "The Giant, Aegaeon." *The Southern Review:* "Adventures in Long Island [No. 1]: The Helpless Detectives," "Modern Romance [Roy Lichtenstein]," "Mrs. Janecek, Inventor of the Telephone." *Willimantic Chronicle:* "Adventures in Long Island [No. 2]: Albert's House," "Proverbs of Birdland."

"Zone 6" appeared in the anthology *Waking Up to the Earth: Connecticut Poets in a Time of Global Climate Crisis* [Grayson Books], edited by Margaret Gibson.

"The Helen of St. Kitts," in another form, was part of the group of poems awarded *Nimrod International Journal's* Pablo Neruda Prize.

"Unrhymed Sonnet between Two Declarative Sentences [No. 1]: S.Z. Leaves for Vietnam" and "Unrhymed Sonnet between Two Declarative Sentences [No. 2]: S.Z. Departs from Troy" appeared under different titles in the chapbook *Mr. Z., Mrs. Z., J.Z., S.Z.* [Ugly Duckling Presse].

Special thanks to Henryk Cierniak, Jim and Helen Coleman, Ginny Connors, Daniel Donaghy, Jessica Faust, Jim Finnegan, Anne Flammang, Debbie Gilbert, Joan Hoffman, Bill LaCapra, David Morse, Nick and Jane Mougey, Margaret Plaganis, Shelley Puhak, Pegi Deitz Shea, Joan Sidney, John Edward Surowiecki, Vanessa and Mike Sylvester, Lisa Taylor, Edwina Trentham and Kate Young.